THE INTENTIONAL FIELD SERVICE ENGINEER

THE INTENTIONAL FIELD SERVICE ENGINEER

Bruce A. Breeden

CONTENTS

INTRODUCTION

Selecting a career as a field service engineer or technician is a rewarding profession in the technical application field. There are opportunities, advancements, and crossover skills for many other careers.

Deciding to develop yourself in this profession will lead to increased pay, more responsibility, promotions, and fulfillment.

Working with purpose, or *intention*, will differentiate you from others and provide for a value-based career and life. Know your values; commit your life to a higher purpose for you, your family, and our world!

Let's get started!

This book is written for you, the field service engineer, field service technician, or someone who is considering this rewarding profession.

Field service engineering spans many industries, technologies, geographies, and types of employers, and the field is growing at above-average rates. There are new job opportunities and career advancement opportunities alike. Even better, field service engineering is also an excellent baseline career for moving into other functional areas using your core skills.

FSE Job Attributes	Job Outlook	Skills
•Independence •Responsibility •Work variation •Interesting •Technology •People •Advancement •Problem solving •Multi-industry •Travel	•Above-average growth •Opportunities •Platform for advancement or transfer to other industries •Experiences and skills of field service engineers also are foundation to transition to other career fields.	•Technical •Electronics •Mechanics •Software •Metrology •Other Core Skills •Customer relations •Service sales •Safety •Productivity and systems •Inventory management

The field service engineer (FSE), while heavily augmented today by remote diagnostic centers and other support structures, is a role that will not be outsourced abroad. A principal responsibility of an FSE is customer relationship, and the value of relationship building is vital to your company's brand and long-term financial equity.

Field service engineering is a core business line of many manufacturers and product distributors that provides a residual revenue stream and close customer relations for future sales, and it is a key element of the corporate quality assurance plan.

Intention is an action word—a word I chose carefully to show you how some practical steps and focus will energize your career and catapult you to new opportunities and advancement. My purpose for this book is to show you opportunities for advancement and for making more income in your career. After thirty-five years in this profession, having the experience as both an FSE and a service executive with many companies and industries, I have lived it, and I know what companies value in field service engineers.

You have to first understand how field service contributes to a corporation's long-term strategic goals and financial outcomes.

Field service engineers have an enormous and measurable impact on a company's overall performance and value. Companies make a large financial investment to establish and operate a field service organization, and as a profit center, the financial and market gain is significant. FSEs should clearly see the connection between a company's strategic objectives and their own contribution. Frankly, this is often clouded in both larger and smaller organizations, but it should never be that way.

Let's use an example. The diagram below shows the direct responsibilities of FSEs or their performance results. While not exclusive, the FSE contributions have a direct impact on the company's overall performance. There are direct impacts of the FSEs and their teams on the organization's results and total company performance. As professional FSEs, we should be clear about as well as proud of our incredible impact on our company's performance.

Company Objectives

- Revenue and profit
- Market share and growth
- New product pipeline
- Customer retention
- Safe, skilled workforce
- Return on assets

Field Service Engineer Contributions

- Build residual service agreement revenue and profit stream.
- Through customer relations, promote products and generate sales leads.
- Provide voice of the customer input and part of product launch success teams.
- Through service and customer relationships, build brand loyalty.
- Conduct travel and work in safe manner, constantly learning new technology and soft skills.
- People and equipment are assets. The very nature of a service business is to operate productively and optimize use of trucks and capital equipment.

Chart 1: FSE's performance alignment to company goals and results

I have dedicated my own professional purpose in life to show you how to grow in a field service career—either by progressing within the field service industry or moving into related careers such as sales and marketing, engineering, manufacturing, quality assurance, customer service, and logistics. Any of these directions is possible, depending on your preferences and experiences.

I encourage you to also read *Intentional Living* by John Maxwell for a broader perspective on living life and determining your personal purpose, which a career is part of. *The Intentional Field Service Engineer* is targeted specifically to those already working as a field service engineer or considering the field.

I have participated in this business for over thirty-five years and have been fortunate enough to work for a few world-class companies with leading field service organizations. After completing an electronics certificate program in the US Air National Guard, I started my field service career at an early age in the biomedical/scientific instrument business. Over my career, my company sponsored my college tuition, and later, my graduate school education, and I relocated a number of times for advancement opportunities. All said, this industry has enabled me to advance to various field service positions, including training and service marketing to global executive leadership. I credit my opportunities to this industry of field service engineering and certainly the great service organizations and people I have been associated with over the years. I've known and worked with plenty of other field service engineers who went into other functions their companies offered, including manufacturing, quality assurance, engineering, software development, marketing, and sales. I am convinced this is a fantastic career field that supports both field service career progression and additional career choices.

Part I of this book will introduce you to the industry and careers of field service engineering. Part II of this book will provide a short overview of the Field Service7, which is a program for how to succeed in this field, and it will provide you the additional growth opportunities of your choice. Part III of this book features profiles of real FSE's who have demonstrated being the Intentional Field Service Engineer and what they have done with their careers in the field service industry.

There are many excellent books, websites, and consultants addressing the business of service, customer loyalty, marketing, and organizational change. This book is not meant to compete with their excellent material or address the same topics. My contention is a two-part point:

1) Field service is critical to a corporation's success. At a manufacturer service organization or an independent distributor service organization, the team of field service engineers and their broad skill sets are the master links to achieving success. Study a company with poor field service or a lack of critical skills, and you will find a decrease in brand equity, market share loss, limited sales growth, and high turnover.

2) The skills of a field service engineer are a unique bundle and provide the foundation of career growth, fulfillment, and rewards.

If you are looking for an industry or profession that you can develop and earn good money in, this is for you. If you are currently working as a field service engineer, field service technician, customer service engineer, and so on, this book will show you how you can excel and transform those skills to either make more money or provide you the pathway to advance to other positions within the service organization or support functions.

PART I

FIELD SERVICE ENGINEERING— THE PROFESSION

CHAPTER 1

BACKGROUND—FIELD SERVICE ENGINEERING

Electronic, mechanical, robotic, and instrument-and-control systems that require on-site installation and maintenance because of their size, expense, installation, or criticality to the site's operation make up the industry called field service engineering.

The role of the field service engineer or technician (FSE) is to provide on-site installation of hardware, software, and peripherals along with operator training. In addition to new equipment installations, the FSE also provides on-site technical service over the life cycle of the equipment, which is typically twelve to fifteen years. This includes

- calibration;
- preventive maintenance;
- hardware and software upgrades; and
- emergency service diagnosis and repairs.

Entry into the field is based on the FSE's technical background, which is often vocational school or an associate's degree in electronics, industrial automation, or biomedical. Entry requirements are mainly based on the industry or type of equipment the FSE will be servicing. For example, industrial machinery used in various production plants normally require more electrical and mechanical skills than can be obtained by experience with a high school education.

The real career differentiators of field service engineers are the sets of professional management skills in addition to the technical skills FSEs exhibit in performing a field role for their company. These professional management skills are

- organization and self-management;
- customer relations;
- inventory management; and
- service-agreement sales.

FSEs are employed directly by the manufacturers of the equipment or their distributors or dealer network. FSEs are also employed by third-party independent service providers that service multiple brands on-site or even in-house by the facility in the maintenance or biomedical departments.

The FSE role provides enormous value to the customer by ensuring their valuable equipment is maintained and properly operating. Most companies run their field service organization as a profit center and rely heavily on the service business line. In many cases, field services are the major revenue- and profit-generating business lines, even more so than new products.

With a technical background in engineering or electronic technology, a person can have responsibility well beyond the laboratory and in-plant bench or maintenance work. Field service engineering is a career of many levels, providing field service support to customers who have electronic and electromechanical equipment, controls, analytical, and process instrumentation at their facility. Usually the equipment is expensive and complex technology that is critical to the customer's operation and requires specialized training, parts, documentation, and test equipment to provide service and support. Most equipment is a system, which includes hardware, firmware, software, peripherals, and a network connection. The FSE's technical responsibility includes installation, commissioning, operator training, preventive maintenance, emergency repair, troubleshooting, software configuration updates, alignments, calibration, and decommissioning.

In addition to the broad yet specialized technical role, the FSE also works in the field to manage a territory and is the primary person responsible for customer relations, service-agreement sales, spare-parts management, service call scheduling, safety, and operation of test equipment and a company vehicle. FSEs usually work as part of a district team of other FSEs or are organized by major product category and work closely with a field administrative-support team, product-sales representatives, and a technical support department.

Depending on a multitude of factors, including the density of the equipment installed in a given geography, technical characteristics of the equipment and application, the price of the equipment, and the volume of service agreements, the territory is staffed with a team of FSEs who provide service and support under a service-agreement relationship. Service agreements are a service product to provide the service operation a profit for staffing, equipping, and training a team of FSEs. In past years, this revenue stream has become extremely profitable and provides a recurring revenue stream that can be far more than revenues from the sale of new products.

An example of this is a piece of equipment that may cost $30,000. After the warranty period, a service agreement may be sold for $1,800 per year, providing preventive maintenance, parts, and repair services. The average life span of this equipment may be ten years. The simple math is $16,200 additional revenue, assuming the first year of service was covered by warranty. Now multiply that by additional product sales that convert to a service agreement, upgrades, and extras, resulting in a bundle of recurring service revenues that will outpace the product sales. In addition, service-agreement customers are typically more satisfied than those who choose to pay as they go in repair-call charges, so the double benefit is that the customer satisfaction drives additional referrals or product sales—more on this subject later.

Another value to having a field service operation is to maintain a strategic partnership with the customer. Providing critical services enhances the value of the installed product and ultimately provides value to the end user's operation as they produce their product or service based on the reliability and effectiveness of the equipment. Senior FSE managers work closely to provide and align technical services with the key customer executives and even consult on future applications and product development projects. This keeps the field service organization intimately involved and critical to the success of their customers and reduces competitive pressures.

Having been in this industry for almost forty years, I want to tell you about both the vertical pathways in field service via the technical or management tracks and also the many complementary fields your skill as an FSE can lead to. Better yet, this book will also provide you with some real-life stories and testimonials from a few FSEs I've had the pleasure of working with. You will see how they thrived in their chosen paths even outside the field service industry.

Technical	Management
Field service technician	Field supervisor/lead FSE
Associate field service engineer	District/territory manager
Field service engineer I, II	Regional manager
Senior field service engineer	Service operations director
Installation engineer	Service training manager
Calibration and validation engineer	Service quality manager
Customer training specialist	Technical support manager
Safety lead	Service parts manager
Applications specialist	Service marketing manager
Field technical specialist	National or global operations director/VP
Technical support specialist	President, service business unit

Chart 2: Typical field-service job positions

These are possible roles within your organization, and they certainly exist in many service organizations or companies. The specific titles may vary from company to company. Again, this is just within the field service organization; later we will talk about how the FSE skills transcend not just field service but in many other careers.

CHAPTER 2

EMPLOYERS AND EMPLOYMENT OUTLOOK

F SEs are employed by equipment manufacturers, distributors, third-party or independent service organizations, and even in-house operations to provide service to their facilities.

A large organization will have hundreds if not thousands of FSEs organized by geography or by product categories to provide timely and proficient field service.

A smaller organization may focus on a specific geography and have just a few FSEs. Still others operate as independent contractors, specializing in a particular product type, or choose to work flexible hours or for projects.

The option of working as an independent contractor or independent FSE is gaining more popularity as FSEs retire. But they still hold a wealth of knowledge and experience, and many are defining a "new deal" retirement plan where they choose their projects, locations, and hours to meet their lifestyles and interests.

The outlook remains above average.

Over one million US workers are employed as field service technicians and engineers with above-average growth prospects, according to the US Bureau of Labor Statistics. Installation, maintenance, and repair occupations are expected to grow 6 percent from 2014 to 2024, resulting in 365,000 new jobs, per BLS.

Field service engineers manage a territory, first in maintaining their assigned line of equipment, but also for service-contract sales and customer satisfaction. Some industry leaders have called FSEs as brand managers based on their degree of impact within a territory to support the company brand and reputation.

There is a certain level of independence that comes from this responsibility in setting your work schedule, making decisions while achieving your productivity, and defining other goals for the company.

Industry areas of field service engineering include

- office/computer equipment;
- biomedical/laboratory equipment;
- clinical chemistry diagnostic analyzers;
- diagnostic imaging;
- optical examination and diagnostic equipment;
- aviation electronics;
- HVAC and controls;
- industrial plant machinery/millwright;
- robotics/automation;

- scientific instrumentation;
- packaging systems;
- diesel machinery;
- hydraulic systems;
- process controls and automation;
- printing systems;
- building automation systems;
- material-handling and material-lifting equipment;
- semiconductor manufacturing systems;
- optical sensing and readers;
- radio/satellite communication;
- security video/point-of-sale computer systems;
- weighing technologies;
- temperature control systems;
- power generation and controls;
- agriculture instrumentation;
- irrigation/water pumping systems; and
- others.

Education/Training Requirements

There is no simple or standard answer, and it primarily depends on the type of the equipment and industry that you are working in. Generally speaking, an AAS degree in technology or military training or experience is the best overall, but the requirements can be lower or higher.

In all cases, the ability to work with test equipment and tools and logically deduce problems is the baseline for entry. Experience is always a formidable complement to any education and sometimes a substitute.

CHAPTER 3

WORKING ENVIRONMENT

Here are a few of the big items to consider:

- inside or outside work
- types of equipment serviced
- industry/customer facilities
- degree of travel
- criticality of equipment
- 24-7 on call
- uniform or dress code
- company vehicle type

As you can imagine, the above industries and technology types greatly vary how the FSE works. Clinical diagnostics FSEs, for example, work primarily in a hospital or a laboratory. Their work on the equipment is 100 percent inside with precise test equipment, small parts, and generally lightweight tools. They wear company logo shirts with casual pants and drive a company car or a small van. In contrast, an industrial machinery FSE is working both inside an industrial plant with machinery and also in outside environments where equipment is located on a site. The tools and equipment are larger, with heavy parts. FSEs may need to do some basic torching and welding as well as troubleshoot complex PLC systems. Because they are working in an industrial environment, they wear work uniforms and safety equipment;

they often get dirty, and they typically drive a utility truck to transport larger tools and equipment.

Travel is usually a large factor for FSEs. The nature of the job is "field" work; you travel from one customer site to another and maybe to the service office. Companies and service organizations greatly vary in the travel requirements, based on their territorial density of installed products and type of products (more specialized v. standard). I once worked for NCR Corporation in the Washington, DC, area, as well as Beckman Coulter. In that area, the density of products was large, and both companies had large district service operations with many FSEs. I never stayed overnight as all my site visits were in the metropolitan area. I transferred with Beckman Coulter to North Carolina, and we only had eight FSEs in a two-state area. I then started traveling and stayed overnight in locations a few hours from my home base once every couple of weeks.

Overnight travel is common in the field service industry but depends on your specific role and organization.

Having worked in the health-care field, I know the urgency and pressure to arrive on-site and correct the problem within just a few hours can be different for many FSEs. Some like the responsibility and pressure while others don't thrive in the 24-7 on-call environment. The money is better, and you really have to be on top of your game to effectively troubleshoot and resolve the problem. Customers depend on it. However, the trend with connected or remote diagnostics–equipped call centers and smart dispatching has helped the FSE enormously. While there is still pressure and responsibility, technology and advance scheduling/parts stocking is helping, and not just in health care. Equipment is used for a purpose, and health care is no different from a large factory operating three shifts around the clock and depending on their industrial equipment. When the equipment is down, it may stop the entire factory. Pressure can be in any of the industry segments, and the ability of the FSE as a problem solver and expert is a very valuable skill to have in the job marketplace.

Your education, training, and industry qualifications have probably guided you on the other working environment factors, but make sure your interests and roles match how you like to work. Most important, be aware of the options, and make sure you have selected or at least targeted the environment that fits you.

My story about entering the field service business

I stumbled into field service after being raised by blue-collar parents—a plumber and a bookkeeper. My father didn't complete high school, opting to enlist in the merchant marines at the end of WWII and then had a career as a plumber and small-business owner. My mother raised four kids and worked full time as a bookkeeper for small businesses. None of my brothers or sister completed college. Being the youngest child, I was curious to do something different—travel and somehow get into a career different from plumbing. I had interest in law enforcement, firefighting, electronics, and aviation.

After high school, I attended a community college, majoring in fire science while working as a volunteer fireman for the county. I wasn't a very dedicated student at the time and wanted to move on with a career, but I had to avoid the family plumbing business. The county had a very long hiring wait for either fire or police department work. I then enlisted in the US Air Force to be a paid firefighter, but they routed me to electronics switching systems school at Sheppard AFB in Texas. Little did I know this would be the beginning of a lifetime career in field service. I started my civilian career in 1979 at an annual salary of a whopping $9,500. I earned twenty-eight credit hours from the US Air Force Community College in electronics and while going back to school during my full-time employment over the years to complete a bachelor's degree in liberal arts and a master's degree in business.

In the course of thirty-seven years in the industry, I have had every job within the service organization:

- associate/field service engineer
- senior field service engineer
- account specialist
- field technical specialist
- district service manager
- service training and technical support manager

- service marketing manager
- service system implementation project manager
- national and global service director
- corporate vice president

I had the benefit of my employer paying for my college education, and equally important I worked with great coworkers and had some great bosses and mentors.

Truly, the journey has been rewarding, with many surprises and equal challenges. Never did I think gaining a technical background would offer me so many opportunities by being a field service engineer.

CHAPTER 4

PERSPECTIVE

When I started my career, the first consideration in finding a job was using my electronics training to provide technical service or assistance for technology. I could have easily started as an engineering technician or in testing in a manufacturing facility. Luckily, I was hired to do field service, which provided me many opportunities to advance with my electronics certificate without having a four-year degree. Here's the point we will build on in this book—the profession of field service is more to do with customer relations, self-management, operator training, service sales, safety, and inventory management than it has to do with technical troubleshooting.

Yes, definitely you need to be highly skilled and proficient in technical expertise. That is a baseline. However, the beauty of the profession is that your role starts with having the technical skill to perform preventive maintenance, read schematics and other technical documentation, know the customer application, and be skilled at advanced troubleshooting and calibration of precision equipment. From that platform, the value provided to the customer and employer is your ability to manage your schedule, develop customer relationships, sell the value of your services, and manage expensive assets like your company's test equipment, spare-parts inventory, and vehicle, while operating safely and as a team player.

Field service engineers have an enormous and measurable impact on a company's overall performance and value. Companies place a very large financial and time investment to establish and operate a field service organization, and as a profit center, the financial and market gain is significant. FSEs should clearly see the connection between a company's strategic objectives to their individual performances. Frankly, this is often clouded in both larger and smaller organizations, and it should never be that way.

Let's use an example. The diagram below shows the direct responsibilities of an FSE or their performance results. While not exclusive, the FSE's contributions directly affect the company's overall performance. There are direct impacts of the FSEs and their team to the organization results and total company performance. As professional FSEs, we should be clear as well as proud of our incredible impact on our company's performance.

Company Objectives

- Revenue and profit
- Market share and growth
- New product pipeline

- Customer retention
- Safe, skilled workforce
- Return on assets

Field Service Engineer Contributions

- Build residual service agreement revenue and profit stream.
- Through customer relations, promote products and generate sales leads.
- Provide voice of the customer input and part of product launch success teams.
- Through service and customer relationships, build brand loyalty.
- Conduct travel and work in safe manner, constantly learning new technology and soft skills.
- People and equipment are assets. The very nature of a service business is to operate productively and optimize use of trucks and capital equipment.

Chart 3: FSE performance alignment to organization or company performance

These concepts will segue into the following chapters of this book about the seven critical elements of an FSE's job. I contend that FSEs who consistently perform and develop within this framework will advance within their company and become more marketable to other companies throughout their careers. In addition, the other career development opportunities are many and varied based on an FSE's specific career interest and areas of expertise.

PART II

FIELD SERVICE7

CHAPTER 5

INTRODUCTION—FIELD SERVICE7

The basis of developing your FSE career is a practical and straightforward concept called the Field Service7. The point is that as an *intentional FSE*, you will personally take charge of your career and options by following a structure that is aligned directly with the success of FSEs and their respective service organizations and companies.

Read on to dedicate yourself to your professional development.

The Field Service7 is specifically designed to identify the seven most critical job categories, where the FSE should maximize his or her performance. This will ultimately lead to increased performance levels, more compensation, and advancement and career marketability. Most important, this is a road map that you can control to determine which career path is best for you.

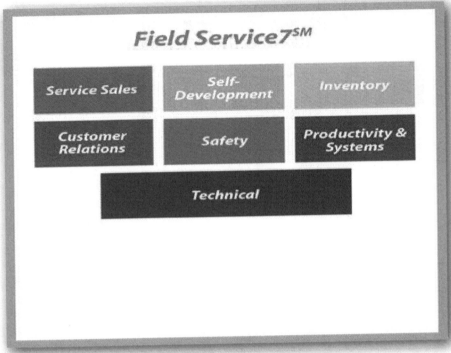

Chart 4: Field Service7

CHAPTER 6

TECHNICAL

FSEs master their assigned products; they are the experts in the room. One of the many challenges to being an excellent FSE is to have a deep experience and knowledge-base of the product based on the customer's usage of the particular equipment or instrumentation. Let's start with the various types of service calls:

- installation
- commissioning
- operator training
- networking between systems
- software applications
- calibration and possible validation/certification
- preventive maintenance
- diagnosis and troubleshooting
- major assembly replacements and alignments
- overhauls/refurbishments
- upgrades and retrofits
- uninstallation

I contend the best FSEs know every aspect of the above service calls. In some cases, junior level or trainees share support responsibility for some of the above call types; however, the path to excellence and advancement is addressing all aspects of service for a particular product. The FSEs who keep this customer-centric vision of their FSE roles will rise ahead of others—either being rewarded by their current company or by demonstrating a much higher degree of expertise to prospective employers.

The FSEs who have an extensive product technical skill usually find themselves being more involved within their company for new-product feedback (voice of the customer), prelaunch testing, being called in to troubleshoot difficult or recurring problem accounts, and training others. These additional roles provide ample opportunity for company recognition, participating in high profile accounts and product teams, and gaining well-earned respect within the company.

Being the expert in the room entails commitment and ongoing development. One can't maintain expert status by learning things once and not keeping up with upgrades, technology changes, and new models within the product family. Most new FSEs don't realize the product line evolution in which ten- to fifteen-year-old product models actually generate the majority of service revenues, but in parallel, new-product models within the same product family are critically important to launch effectively to recoup the R&D costs. The result in field service is that the organization is responsible for all ages of product support, cradle to grave, and it is often quite a challenge to adapt to new technology while maintaining expertise in old technology and practices.

Professional FSEs maintain their technical documentation, whether printed manuals, bulletins, or electronic documentation systems. I have worked with many FSEs who seldom read and truly digest tech bulletins. This is a terrible mistake as part of being a professional FSE is resourcefulness and ensuring documentation, test equipment, and calibration tools are used to properly complete the tasks—and in a timely fashion.

A few words of caution about technical expertise: A wise technical instructor once taught me the FSE's overall job is to fix the customer and not just the instrument. We can easily get carried away and not effectively listen to the complaint. We may immediately go to work and take the cover off and begin tinkering. This same instructor also said that upon arriving at the customer's site, leave your tool bag in the hallway while you talk to the customer about the problem, and then operate the equipment. These were wise words. There have been times when I have hurried along, eager to take care of the problem, and missed some obvious clues.

Always remember the importance of customer interaction and relationship development. This is often with multiple customers and different personalities and roles within one account site.

We will talk about customer relations in the next chapter, but for now, remember that your customer is a human, and not a piece of equipment or a machine.

The technical skill that FSEs provide, combined with their mastery on their assigned product lines, is the core skill of the Field Service7 and is also the foundation of the other six skills.

Maintaining technical skills through major technological advances is one of the most challenging aspects of the FSE job, especially since there are always variations in service as products age in the territory's installed base.

Congratulations! You have started in this field with a technical background, training, and skills. With a commitment to maintain and continuously grow in your technical profession, these skills will continue to serve you well.

Field Service 7
Technical Action Items

1. Master your subject—your assigned product lines. It's probably a lot of various models over the years, even various brands.
2. Know the different types of service calls for these products and how to master the steps to complete each one.
3. Often the customer training, applications support, and programming are the highest perceived values of the customer experience. Develop yourself to master those roles for advancement.
4. Maintain your documentation and links, and complete the updates to have the most up-to-date version of your reference material, including technical bulletins.
5. Troubleshooting begins with listening to the customer and the equipment.
6. Use your resources, senior FSEs, technical support, and diagnostic tools.
7. Commit to a career of technology development, and embrace new technology with continued learning and curiosity.
8. Always prepare before arriving on-site or speaking to the customer about the problem. Professional FSEs review documentation and check their tools and equipment to make sure they are updated and prepared for the service call.
9. Always ask: Am I prepared to be the expert in the room? Am I worth what the customer is paying for the service agreement or hourly rate?

CHAPTER 7

CUSTOMER RELATIONS

The best part of being a field service engineer is the responsibility you have in that role to develop strong customer relationships. This is a huge responsibility. Please remember that your role while interfacing with the customer by e-mail, phone, or on-site is to represent your entire company. You hear a lot about brand development in business. FSEs are part of the brand. Companies spend millions of dollars on brand development; they speak of it as "brand equity," and it is true and critical. However, when you are doing your job, the customer sees you as the entire company and the brand. Please remember and respect this part of the FSE job. This is the number-one differentiator of service organizations and FSEs alike. Seize the opportunity and develop these skills the best you can.

Bottom line is people do business with people they like and trust. This is the most important part of field service because no matter what your level of expertise is, or what you bring in specialized equipment, parts, factory support, and so on, if the customer's experience with you is negative, then all efforts are wasted. These subtleties and perceptions tell you why the customer chose your service or someone else's in your own organization or a competitor.

You not only represent the brand for your company, but in many cases, you are also the brand.

Excelling as a field service engineer involves putting yourself in the customer's shoes. We talked earlier about being the "expert" in the room. The rest of the story is about using that expertise in a careful, deliberate way that exudes both confidence and courtesy. Usually, listening and empathy are the perfect characteristics that will leverage your knowledge to communicate effectively with your customer.

Remember, first put your tool bag down and go listen to the customer. Hear what the problem is in a professional, patient, and inquisitive manner. After the call is completed, you need to use some of their same words and descriptions in response as you go over their description of the symptom or problem. People want to be heard. As humans we have a terrible habit of speaking over each another in our daily lives, assuming that we know what others are going to say. As professionals, we need to let the other people complete their sentences and repeat back what we heard.

Since you are an expert on their system, you can then confidently provide answers to the customer on what you found, the options, and an action plan all based on first hearing what they had to say. If a customer directly asks you what you think the problem is, it's fine to provide a direct answer, but always qualify your answer with words and phrases like typically, generally, or before I check this out myself. Or you could reference a document, and so on.

Proactive communications is a must. Never let the customer have to call you for a follow-up. Be the action-based and conscientious FSE who commits and actually makes the follow-up phone call or e-mail inquiry. It shows you care and are responsible for their situation, even if you have to escalate the problem to others.

Remember you are the guest at the customer's facility. Always act with courtesy; ask if you can use their desk space or make phone calls from your service location. You may be disruptive without even knowing it. Be grateful you're at their site. Don't think that they should be grateful that you are there to solve their problem. It's a mind-set, and as the saying goes, "an attitude of gratitude" goes a long way.

Getting to know your repeat customers is always beneficial, but you have to play that by ear, depending on your industry or specific customer personality. It's easy to go overboard and unknowingly take up too much of their time. We all know the vendor who shows up on-site and talks your ear off—from traffic to sick kids to, worst of all, complaining about his or her company! Remember who you work for—again, it's about gratitude and professionalism. Sure, we all have our problems, including our own company. But as a professional FSE, never, ever—I repeat; never, ever—share dirty laundry with customers. There's a time and place for everything, but there is no better way to run off a customer than to slam your employer, your boss, or company's products.

Keep the big picture of customer relations in mind:

- Communicate, communicate, and communicate—proactively.
- Dress to look the part.
- Listen, repeat, and discover.
- Prepare, have the right tools, documents, and parts.
- Be the guest in the house. Be courteous and neat.
- Get to know the customers, their businesses, and processes.
- Be grateful and thankful. Smile and introduce yourself often.
- Provide clear options and action pathways to solve their problems.
- Escalate quickly if you need help—your customer and company will appreciate it!
- Be the professional in the room with your expertise, resources, product knowledge, and promotional material.
- Never talk badly about your company or the competition.

I could write an entire book about selling services, but here is one key point worth noting. We will just touch on it briefly in the upcoming chapter on service sales. Customer accounts are full of different buying roles. You need to know at the very least that there are technical influencers as well as economic influencers within the account, and the combination of the two will determine whether your company does business with them for their product and service needs.

The technical influence is closest to your daily contacts that operate the equipment and instrumentation you are servicing. They concern themselves with the operation and usage of the systems. The economic influencers may be the department heads or purchasing agents. Obviously the buyers are mostly concerned with the cost of service, downtime, and buying and maintaining the systems they buy and use. In your role as a professional FSE, always try to identify these influencers and remember to speak their language. For example, if I service an instrument and install an engineering retrofit, I express to the technical influencers how this will improve the operation of the system or remove a programming bug. On the economic side, I discuss how this retrofit will reduce downtime or is included in the cost of their service agreement.

One perspective of customer satisfaction is that we can look at a service call as a simple transaction between the FSE and the customer.

Instrument down to instrument up: simple as that.

The hours and parts are billed or charged against a contract, and the customer transaction is complete.

Transactions never earn business, however; trusted relationships between people do.

The right perspective is to look at a service call as a continuation of your relationship with the customer, which equals value.

Value defines who gets the customer's business for the long run. A service call is a huge opportunity to generate value through relationships, and the various call types are all opportunities to excel at building customer relationships. Remember, the Saturn car company in the eighties? They were well known for changing the entire automobile industry by making car buying a "celebration event" and beginning a relationship with a customer. Saturn car dealerships were filled with photos of happy buyers, sometimes buying their first new car. They championed the event and promoted a satisfied experience. They changed the normal shopping-and-closing transaction to that of a customer relationship. In our world, that could be an installation, preventive maintenance, emergency repair, or upgrade type of call. Each customer contact is an opportunity to establish and reinforce value.

Recognize the best practices of other companies, including how one employee made a difference in your experience. Ask yourself what you can do today to make the customer experience different and exceptional? Do this consistently, and you will surely be rewarded in many ways. I don't mean discounting or giving away services—that only erodes the value of your expertise and function—but instead really caring about your customers and their problems, and making the problem-solving process positive.

Professional FSEs understand the dynamics of customer accounts and relationships. They team with their fellow FSEs and sales representatives to develop strong relationships with their customers and look at and practice their craft as a complete professional. The secret to career advancement begins with customer relationships, and you can ask the CEO of any company about that too—I bet he or she will tell you it is still critically important, even in the executive role.

Let the above be guiding principles to advance yourself and your organization. How you act and interact with customers heavily influences your entire company's brand, customer loyalty rating, and your personal career growth. Earn the customer's respect, and that will drive your career.

Field Service7
Customer Relations Action Items

1. Always remember that you represent the company brand and are a brand in itself.
2. Proactive communication is a must. Don't let a customer have to call you for information and updates.
3. Listen, listen, and listen.
4. Be exceptional in your customer care today.
5. Build relationships and transcend basic transactions.
6. Service trumps discounts.
7. Dress as a professional FSE. You are on stage.
8. You are a guest at their facility. Be courteous and polite.

CHAPTER 8

PRODUCTIVITY AND SYSTEMS

The international language of business is productivity. You need to know that and recognize the clear fact that productivity matters to your employer, the viability of your service business, and the customer's interpretation of the value received from your service. Own this part in your career, and if your company's "methods and systems" are obstacles to productivity, then you should provide suggestive solutions or ask to participate in process improvement. Really, you need to own this and lead by example.

The economics of a field service organization is the same as a factory in terms of quantity and quality of work produced in a given time frame. The service business is simply based on hours, maximizing the "productive" time to total available time. There are 2,080 work hours, or "total" time in a given year. Each organization has different policies and metrics, but the basic principle is the same. How did the FSE maximize his or her time in a given year relative to established business objectives and measurements?

$$\frac{\text{Productive time: labor, travel charged to contracts, time and material charged call}}{\text{Total available time: 2,080 hours per year}} = \text{Productivity}$$

Example: The FSE has 1,550 total labor and travel hours of installation, customer training, applications support, diagnostics, adjustments, repair, and parts replacement activity in the year, which is either charged against warranty, contract, demo equipment, or time and material to the customer.

$$\frac{1,550 \text{ hours}}{2,080} = 74.5\% \text{ productive time}$$

It is critical to thoroughly understand what productivity means to your organization. Service organizations don't expect 100 percent productive time from an FSE. Obviously, vacation, illness, training, customer relations, service selling, and internal meetings round out the rest of the available time. In most cases, service organizations will have productivity goals representing the need to make good use of the FSE's time by completing service calls both effectively and efficiently.

Some organizations may take productivity measurements further by tracking time per call, percentage of travel time to labor time, and even service quality elements, including callback percentage and parts stocking percentage. These are all customary and critical to operating a good business and achieving customer objectives. The FSE's job is to make sure he or she completely understands the metrics and the why behind the objectives and to exceed company productivity goals. As systems, management, or the business climate changes, expect an update or complete change to productivity metrics.

In my experience, productive time was measured as described above for a "contract" model service business. Over time, FSEs were incentivized by productive time to charge more service time to contracts. This became a problem as contract time increased per management's direction, but with the invention of competitive service organizations, my employer realized that they had been increasing the price of the contracts to the customers to cover the "productive time" consumed. This slowly led prices to be uncompetitive.

Not all product lines, FSE roles, and geographies are the same. Allowances or desired objectives need to address the true factors of providing service and support to a product and the practical geographic factors in remote or metropolitan areas.

Eventually, we ended up measuring the profit of the contracts down to the district and FSE level and throughout the traditional methods. In addition, we measured customer contract retention so the contract profitability and customer retention balanced each metric and provided the positive change in productivity and doing the right thing for the customer. That change provided FSE discretion, proficiency, and customer relationship factors to the service product and further added to the point of the criticality of the FSE skills and effectiveness for the business results.

This may all sound confusing now, but it's not—just recognize the company's objectives for productivity and be part of the success. Productivity accomplishment is a key to progressing in your career as a professional FSE. Now let's peel the onion a bit on other factors involved in achieving your objectives and standing out among your peers.

It's important to recognize the dynamics of obtaining productivity within the field service industry. Productivity is not obtained by simply working harder and longer, but by a combination of factors:

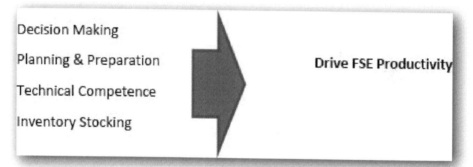

Decision Making

Planning & Preparation

Technical Competence

Inventory Stocking

Drive FSE Productivity

FSEs utilize these and other factors to make good decisions on a daily basis while meeting customer expectations. This is an incredible dynamic that results in a good use of time and resources to accomplish the service task. In our profession—and being accountable for the customer interaction—the buck stops here, and the impact is huge.

The FSE can easily get buried by a problem and not escalate an issue. In the last chapter, we covered the need to know your resources and the right time to call for help so as to not let a simmering fire fester or explode. In general, here are the main scenarios to avoid:

- Not having the correct spare part (commonly used) that requires a second trip. Inventory is expensive, and we can't stock everything. Predetermining part requirements for the equipment installed base or service-agreement population must be undertaken. Typically it is through a combination of management reports showing usage, recommended quantity stocking, and FSE discretion.
- Not calling for help when you are going nowhere fast in diagnosing and repairing a system. We have all been there. We may be confident and logical, but there are just those problems and systems that eat our lunch. Don't delay in calling for help.
- Not being prepared and not calling the customer—we'll discuss more of that below.

Another important decision is whether to stay over and wait for an overnight part or return home and have more travel time. I can't provide examples for all the scenarios, but let's say you are two hours away. If you have to overnight the part, it's probably best to stay overnight, with the cost of lodging and meals versus going home and having the two-hour drive the next day. This is particularly wise if you can do another call while you are waiting for the part to arrive.

Now, this is a typical practical decision that professionals make every week or even daily. Variables to this decision are company policy, customer expectations, response time, other call considerations, getting order confirmation that FedEx has really shipped it, location, and many other factors. There is no single correct answer. But a professional FSE considers all of that, including personal factors such as home care, their kids' activities, and other commitments. If you see I am building the case that a field service engineer or technician is different from a shop-based person, you are right!

Planning and Preparation

This is so important to managing your time and maximizing your effectiveness as an FSE.

Prepare before arrival of the arrival. Make sure that you have the other key items besides parts: all tools, service manual, tech bulletins, test equipment, correct address and contact information, site entry requirements, and so on. I can remember plenty of FSEs who went back to their vehicles as many as ten times during one call to keep getting things. It's really the little things, and I certainly have learned my own lessons over the years and paid each time—usually my own time and money!

Make sure you call ahead to let them know you are coming. Do some planning; make sure you can get into the site or building, get a parking space, have the right tools and equipment, and reassure the customer. If the call is a new installation and includes customer training, this is the time to double check that all site requirements have been met, and make sure the customer understands the scheduling and is prepared for the operator training.

In past years when I was an FSE, productivity varied from total "productive" hours against a contract or warranty and billable calls to even just measuring territory profit. They are both good measurements; it is the FSE's job to understand how productivity is defined and measured by their organization. In general, an outstanding FSE "produces" for the organization as measured by

- calls completed within requested time (both emergency repairs and preventive maintenance);
- calls completed within expected time frames based on product type and task;
- calls reported as complete while at site, information entered online, or paperwork submitted daily;
- travel time minimized by route scheduling, parts stocking, and completion of preventive maintenance calls while at the sites;
- callbacks minimal due to recurring issues or part shortages;
- new service contract sales or product leads generated;
- training, fleet maintenance, inventory completed in prompt, thorough, and accurate manner; and
- relationships with customers developed in idle time and courtesy calls or e-mail contacts conducted in idle time.

Technical Competence

I will not repeat all the information discussed earlier, but you should recognize the practical need for just-in-time (JIT) training. As usual, field service calls can be quite diverse and surprising. A typical preventive maintenance (PM) call may seem routine until you arrive there and find a unique accessory or program running. Emergency repair calls are all over the place, and installations and customer training have their own set of variables. Expect the unexpected and work hard at gaining information or quick tutorials before arriving on-site. That is not the place to figure it out and wing it. Many service organizations have online training tools and resources to help you along. I found it impossible years ago to know everything on a broad line of product service responsibilities, so I used quick reference material to help me along and be productive.

Inventory Stocking

As times get leaner, circuit boards and EPROMS are more specialized; inventory stocking becomes the great enabler to productivity. I was taught and given a manual system of parts management when I started as an FSE. This was a religion within my service organization, and we FSEs didn't care to do it, but it was vital to our success and customer satisfaction. Of course, we can't carry a massive load of parts due to cost, space, and specialization of software and components. So we must do our best to stock what should support our equipment responsibilities within our geographies and actively manage inventory as we do in using our car to be on-site. This isn't the chapter in inventory management, but please recognize the importance of proper inventory management to productive time. They go hand in hand, much like technical competence.

To summarize, productivity is an art and a science, and the FSE who excels at maximizing productivity will advance within an organization because there is never a more critical and clear performance metric than productivity.

People in the organization who explain how busy they are have always amused me. Interestingly, these same people always have the plenty of time to talk your ear off and tell you and many others just how busy they are! Don't be like that—use your skills in planning, preparation, and using resources to be productive.

Congratulations! You understand your organization's productivity model and maximize your time with preparation, planning, and good decision making. Please recognize and understand your specific service organization's goals and metrics. This is clearly the first step. Second, always be mindful and practice the factors that influence your productivity within your organization, practices, and products serviced: decision making, planning and preparation, technical competence, and inventory management. Finally, keep focused on the goals and act on the decision making, planning, technical, and inventory to realize productive time improvement. You will clearly benefit within your organization or elsewhere by demonstrating your effective use of time and exceeding your goals.

Field Service 7
Productivity Action Items

1. The saying is true. Time is money.
2. Productivity is created by proper preparation, planning, and decision making.
3. Know your company's productivity model; this can vary greatly, depending on your equipment type, industry, and business model.
4. Inventory stocking is critical to productivity.
5. Expect the unexpected. Know your exit strategy for problems.
6. The key to operating as an FSE is organization and self-management, which drives productivity in conjunction with customer relations and good decision making.
7. Entering call times, service reports, hours worked, and service inventory into the service management system, all keep the transactions and information flowing from the field through the various company departments. Until your data is entered via your mobile device, it never happened.

CHAPTER 9

SAFETY

There is no such thing as a service business without you. If you get hurt, the costs to the business are enormous—you are absent from serving your customers, the cost of care and treatment, insurance, and paperwork. Accidents can also be painful or fatal. The suffering could extend well beyond you to your family, friends, and co-workers. No matter what industry you are in, field service engineers must work safely and be well trained and proficient in safety.

As mentioned earlier, field service is a business line for an organization that provides continual stream of revenues and profits to the company. The service business is significant to the larger corporation. We are a service business, meaning our product is people. I like to think of us humans in the service business as vehicles and planes from time to time. Think of your effectiveness in terms of transportation. We are not very useful when we do not transport to a customer's site by car, truck, or airplane. When the car, truck, or plane breaks down or is in an accident, we basically can't do our jobs. And if we have a bad driving record, a company will not hire us as an FSE. Based on this example, think of the safety and wellness with regard to your company's vehicle and driving record. If an accident occurs, your productivity, customer responsiveness, and your well-being all stops immediately. This in turn hinders the service business and can result in millions of dollars a year in costs to the service organization, a business operation that is critical to the entire corporation.

We hear about safety and wellness from many perspectives. This is especially true in recent years with the spiraling cost of health care, increased workplace regulation (anybody been to a chemical production facility lately?), the legal world of workman's compensation, and the constant pre-employment and current employment screenings. These are all realities and important, but FSEs are practical-thinking professionals. Just think of it as common sense:

- Who wants to get hurt and be in pain or have a tragic accident or hurt others?
- Who wants to lose a job and career opportunity?
- Who wants to work for a hazardous company?
- Who wants to pay higher insurance premiums and medicine prices?

Create your own list. Think of the macro level consequences of safety and wellness to you and your family. No matter what type of equipment you are working on—moving parts, electrical current, the sample within, the instrument, or the facility itself—all have safety hazards and constant exposures for you to be injured. Look at how many miles we drive a year and think about the statistical probability of being involved in a driving accident. Not to mention driving in other cities or in inclement weather. I have many experiences of driving a rental vehicle in a strange city, trying to follow a map or GPS, while a winter storm is unleashed. The hardships are real, and they are common.

Wellness is a broad subject that I will not go into from a medical standpoint since I am not a medical professional. However, common sense tells us that we must listen to the medical people who talk about the need to address our individual health and live a healthy lifestyle and utilize the preventive checkups and tests provided in our insurance plans.

The beginning points of the chapter, safety and wellness, are part of the Field Service7 because professional FSEs take responsibility for this part of their job and simply can't be effective in doing their job without conducting it in a safe manner and not being present due to illness. Technical competence and customer relationship skills, safety, and wellness are developed skills and are a measureable part of the job. This is especially important in the field service profession, because you are working in the field alone and unsupervised, and you are exposed to countless risks and exposures. We often see large one-hundred-ton cranes mounting equipment thousands of feet in the air onto rooftops. We think of how dangerous the work environment is with the apparatus, height, weight, and risks to the workers. Did you know those are some of the safest workers in the industrial world? Why? Because they are working as a team with dedicated safety spotters, excellent defined training and equipment for each worker, and work procedures that are designed specifically for the task at hand relative to the known exposures.

Now think of your life as an FSE. You travel to various sites, the site is relatively unknown to you, the equipment varies throughout the day, you typically work alone and have a general level of safety training but nothing exactly for the task(s) that you are doing. These differences clearly show the exposures an FSE has during each and every day; basically the crane example is a controlled environment that is engineered for safety. They take an incredibly hard and dangerous job and provide the environment and engineering to drastically reduce the risk. Why? Because they have learned through some extremely tragic circumstances and accidents where lives have been lost or ruined. And there have been examples of this in field service too, and it is our job to control our environment and engineer the process to prevent accidents.

Now you may be thinking that your specific industry is not a heavy-industrial or large-machinery environment. Don't be fooled into thinking you have inherent advantages or reduced risks. Actually, like the comparison above, these environments are often the safest because of the known exposures and thorough training and work plans to reduce those risks. The other day an FSE told me he would much prefer to work in the large chemical plants than on equipment located in agricultural sites. He said that at the chemical company, they have strict standards and observers, and everyone respects safety and safe work practices. Whereas in contrast, he is often out in a rural area and is required to work alone, going into dark, deep pits to service the equipment, where numerous hazards exist.

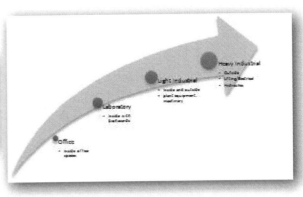

Chart 5: Safety risk

Field service, no matter what industry, has these inherent risks:

- working on light or heavy-duty machinery, electrical and mechanical assemblies that have electrical current, moving objects, heat, and sharp edges
- equipment and instrumentation that is used in production, laboratory, and outside environments
- medical and life science fields that have radiation, blood-borne pathogens, bodily fluids, and animal specimens
- transportation—driving lots of miles visiting customer sites with a higher probability for having a traffic accident; driving in unfamiliar cities or even countries with different traffic patterns, laws, languages, and car types; driving unfamiliar rental vehicles; following GPS instructions while driving; distracted driving with potential company communication on cell phone and texting
- after-hours work and stress factors in completing calls, difficult problems, and working long hours
- always working at a customer's facility and not being familiar with site, environment, and methods of operation
- operating machinery, power tools, or large apparatus

- lifting, bending, and other ergonomic issues
- winter-summer weather issues, driving in inclement weather, slips and falls on ice, and heat and cold exposure

I am sure all of these look familiar to you in your difficult repair assignments and environments.

The key step is to *engage* in your company's safety program. Management has no chance to have a successful safety program without your engagement. Engagement in this sense means to really believe the merits behind the safety argument and take full accountability for your training, decision making, and daily work practices to be different.

An organization with people who understand the argument and are truly engaged in being safe makes all the difference in having a successful program or not. This is not just company slogans, banners, memos, and plaques on the wall. You can train a fully engaged organization because people there talk and act differently. People in unengaged organizations joke about safety and after the safety manager leaves, they go back to their own way of doing things. They do not really believe in the safety rules or holding one another accountable. I liken it to a company with poor product quality, and we in service really know how that can make all employees and customer suffer. An assembly associate can't shut the production line down. When the management really doesn't care about them—just about getting the widget built and shipped—people go about their jobs like robots. People work with their heads down, and the turnover is high, but somehow when things go wrong, fingers abound to point to who screwed up.

- Engaged operations are the first learning organizations. People gather to gain new insights and skills to do things better as a form of quality. Training is an investment and a valued time commitment with resultant improvement in performance; it is not drudgery and another "corporate program" to endure.
- Members of engaged operations help one another, and employees are not just empowered but encouraged to speak up and identify issues with constructive ideas and suggestions to

improve, even if it hinders the service for a time until the quality deviation is corrected.

- Engaged organizations aspire to know the score and truly win. They are a group of people who represent quality in all that they do, knowing how their accomplishments result in the greater fulfillment of company's mission and that they will share in these rewards.

In summary, safety is a critical element of the service operation from both a human and a business objective standpoint. Those two elements can't be separated, and safety performance addresses both. You, the professional FSE, play a critical part in accomplishing these goals, and you must engage and demonstrate proficiency in safety to grow and prosper as an FSE.

Field Service 7
Safety Action Items

1. Engage in your company's safety plan, ask questions, communicate, and challenge.
2. Slow down and be aware; look around, and be cognizant of the risks.
3. Driving is part of our job, not just in our own car and in our own town, but often while traveling in unfamiliar vehicles and roads. You are far more likely to have an accident than others, and that demands extra caution.
4. Make sure you have the correct personal-protection equipment and the right tools for the job. Know how to use them!
5. Think about safety as you start your day and during each call. Preparing for your service calls should always include thinking about the safety risks and actions, just like knowing about what equipment and parts to bring along.
6. You are in control of your safety.
7. Avoid the pain and suffering, as well as the possible absence from your job.
8. Teamwork and cooperation are critical to working as a safe FSE.
9. Safety metrics are just as important as revenue, profit, customer satisfaction, and the rest of the business metrics.
10. Remember: no FSE, no customer, no service business, no career.

CHAPTER 10

SERVICE SALES

After technical knowledge, service sales is the next most critical element to the Field Service7. Recognize first that we all sell every day. It doesn't mean we have "sales representative" on our business card. The secret to selling and gaining revenue is in understanding your role as a field service professional—you are responsible to solve the problems by using all of your resources and to recommend solutions. You need to change your mind-set. Being a service representative is a glorious and fulfilling way to professionally solve your customers' problems, but being recognized (and paid) as a revenue generator for your company is also important to your career. The saying "Service sells" is certainly true and very rewarding.

We should take the word "sales" out of our vocabulary. We get too hung up on the role of selling. Visualize yourself as a company representative who is on-site in front of various customers. By the very nature of being on-site in front of the customer's equipment and personnel, you are selling. First, you are selling yourself as part of the company's brand. We have discussed about this earlier in customer relations. My point is that selling services is not selling in the typical context; instead we are listening, communicating, explaining, demonstrating, and above all, servicing our customer's needs. The fact of the matter is that your counterparts in product or application sales do exactly the same thing. It doesn't matter whether we are talking about products or services; the process of selling is the same. What's helpful though, is that in the field service profession, you can talk about what you know in providing customer support, and effortlessly position your company's range of services to fit the needs of your customer. I clearly believe service sells. So focus on your service levels and the following points, and transform your efforts and successes.

Without a steady stream of revenue from selling your company's service-agreement programs and parts, there is no service organization. We have discussed about the importance of a service organization for the growth of a company's overall business. It is the service sales and revenues that create the profits and continual stream of revenue that make service so important to the bottom line of a corporation. You, as a professional FSE, make a huge difference both in obtaining new service sales and in retention of the current customer base.

Before we go further, let's start with the business background of retention and new business. See diagram in chart 6 below. The bucket represents the existing customer base of business. For example, let's say in your territory, the base of business represents $1 million of service-agreement revenues.

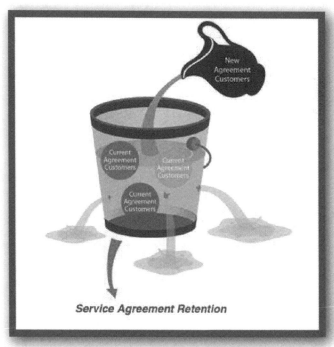

Chart 6: Service-agreement retention

Now, there is a reality that in any given period, customers will naturally leave your territory through no fault of your own. Some customers will go out of business; some will move their operation away from your area; some will simply have less money to keep their operation running from year to year; some will die; and some will—you get the point. Look at the holes in the bucket. These signify openings in your bucket that will leak dollars.

Other holes represent market or self-inflicted damages to the container. These represent competitive losses, dissatisfied customers, obsolescence, and so on. These are the holes we control. Sometimes there are absolutely none in a given year, while other times there's a bit of a flood. When it floods, the ship can sink, and it can certainly take a detour to correct itself and get back on course.

- So the first job in service sales is to keep the accounts you currently have your outstanding levels of service and customer satisfaction. A good marketing department will leverage product obsolescence to not only replace aging products in the field but also offer new and more service features for newer products. This does not just induce a trade-in to newer technology but also increases the service revenues. You and your service engineer colleagues are the most critical element of customer and contract retention. Customers buy things based on their confidence and comfort with the specific service representatives of the company. Let that be you.
- The second job in service sales is to convert the new customers to your service program. So if you want to look smart in front of your service management team, ask about how it is going for both the "renewal" rate and the "conversion" rate of your service-agreement business. Any service business needs to excel at both. With natural causes, a renewal rate can never be 100 percent, so there has to be an overcompensation of new business conversions to not just stay even but to improve the service business year over year. Companies will also implement price increases, which will help the renewal base of business, but a good service-marketing

department measures all factors of the business including unit renewals, price increase, new service units sold, dollar amount of new service-agreement units sold, average net realized price per service agreement, and finally overall service sales of agreements, time and material, parts, and other services. While you are servicing your customers' equipment, be it at installation or during any in-warranty service, they should know about all the various post-warranty support options your company offers. In order to do service for the customers, you should have a starting point of the service needs in your mind, based on how the customers are using the equipment and the level of criticality of the equipment within the operation.

- Spend time getting to know about the key personnel operating or in charge of the equipment.
- Figure out who makes the decision to buy a service contract or in general makes the financial decisions of maintenance and support.
- Define service needs relative to
  - frequency of use;
  - hours of usage (24-7?);
  - response time;
  - environment;
  - criticality—primary or backup equipment;
  - cost consciousness;
  - administrative process to issue a purchase-order number for emergency repair calls;
  - quantity of operators or turnover; and
  - calibration and regulatory requirements.

Based on your clear understanding of how they operate their equipment and specific account requirements, you are now intimately familiar with *their* needs and concerns. Now you can address each one in the proposed service packages that your customers need to best fit their businesses and provide them options in the choice of service programs. See how this is not selling?

Your customers will appreciate your concern in addition to your role of being a technician on-site who comes and goes. And believe me, your company will love it!

Besides positioning and recommending service solutions, your opportunity and role is to provide product-sales leads to your company's counterparts in sales. In most companies, the field service engineers far outnumber product-sales representatives, and you have more access to direct customers. Regardless, you should use your access and knowledge to help your sales representatives.

First, customer service is paramount to selling products. A piece of equipment has a life cycle, and if replacement or additional equipment is involved, customers choose whether to buy again solely based on service and product performance. Again, you, the field service engineer, have a huge influence on that decision. So start with respecting your role and providing great service. As you encounter equipment aging or performing poorly relative to a customer's needs, you become the eyes and ears of the sales force, and you should be providing insight, directing leads and information to sell more products. Even your customer will appreciate your concerns and suggestions as a trusted adviser. Now, don't cross the line and dominate your time and the customer's time with pushy sales. Again, you are there to be intimate with their needs and circumstances, and you should always be perceived as the support person.

There is a beautiful thing about services—yes, you can sell services, and you can also sell services simply by providing great services to your customers. I really want you to remember that. It will be our foundation to further refine our skills if we speak as an FSE in selling services.

Too often, FSEs get uptight about the word "sell." Not everyone wants to sell for a living and deal with rejection, cold calling, being pushy, competitive, and so on. And of course, you have heard or even said yourself, "I was hired to service, not sell." In some cases, we have too much work, and we need to move on to the next service call. Once you get the mindset to differentiate yourself as an FSE with the Field Service7, as well as to differentiate your company and its wide range of services, you will soon plan to spend the right time with the right customers to talk about their service needs.

Let's start with recognizing your company's services. These could be parts, service-agreement programs, extended-warranty programs, upgrades, operator training, relocation/reinstallation, and documentation; professional services such as applications, validation, engineering support, and project management. Chances are your organization can provide either part or all of these services, depending on your industry and company. The offerings also vary depending on whether you work for a manufacturer, distributor, third party, or independent service organization, or even in-house support to internal departments. What do you know about incentive plans, literature, marketing tools, YouTube, podcasts, and your company's Internet communications and other social media? The pace of information flow and design of new programs is fast and sometimes we miss things without being proactive. You should take an inventory of all the services, internal policies and incentives, understand how your company positions and promotes these services, and finally learn new ways to sell and get paid for generating leads or closing sales. So job number-one is to understand all your service products that are marketed and how to effectively use all the provided tools and literature to make money.

Key Fact

Most manufacturing or product-sales organizations want to expand their services to have over 25–50 percent of their total revenues coming from their services. In addition, most companies prefer service revenue in the form of service agreements, which is a consistent stream of monthly revenue that is easier to forecast and plan for staffing and training levels than cyclical time-and-material-based transactions.

You and your support teams *are* the product. The more effective, responsive, and professional your service level is to the customer, the easier it is to generate service revenue and sign customers up for your support services. And here lies a key point. Please understand that you are selling yourself and your company's support level, not some product and key features. So be the best in service. Simply start with communicating how you and your teammates will—and do—provide service to solve the customer problems. If you are proud of your service, you can also proudly communicate (fancy marketing people call this "positioning") how you will do so for your customer. That is our form of selling.

I strongly believe the key to selling services is to make sure you understand what the customers' needs are or what they want to have. This means to quit talking and politely ask probing questions to your customer. Give them the courtesy of asking what they require to use the equipment or instrumentation you are servicing relative to their operation. Obviously, the needs could vary by equipment type, age, criticality within operation, customer budget, hours of operation, and personnel. You must be sure to listen and take notes. Repeat back what you heard to the customer from time to time to verify you understood those needs or concerns.

Always be prepared. Have literature or other marketing tools on hand. If you e-mail your customer, provide a convenient link to your website, Facebook, YouTube, podcast, and so on, or attach a brochure or quotation. Any professional FSE is prepared, just like when he or she is doing a service diagnostics call. Often the customer will want a reference or an example of another customer with a similar support plan. Start to develop your reference list. Again, great service provides for great service sales. Always take care of your customers and they will gladly be the reference for your next sale.

Congratulations in being the complete FSE professional. Having technical skills combined with strong customer relationships is a value that a customer is willing to spend for your services and the support structure your company provides. You don't sell; you service and build relationships that generate valuable revenue for your company and teammates.

To summarize, *selling service* is doing great service and problem solving. Don't think of yourself as needing to be a super salesperson. Customers buy from people whom they respect and like being around. Keep it simple, do great service, go the extra mile, and communicate what your company offers and how the customer can take the next step.

Field Service7
Service Sales Action Items

1. Solving problems is not limited to troubleshooting the equipment. It could be the contract coverage options, cost, and other customer concerns about their equipment.

2. Selling services starts with selling yourself and the services you provide. Remember, service is intangible; you have to show the value of services provided.

3. Recognize that the recurring revenue stream generated by the service-contract business is critical and valued by your company.

4. Understand the value of a customer and the contract retention concept in chart 6 versus the leaking bucket. Be sure to first work on keeping your current contract customers whom you can add on to with the new customers. New customers come from expiring warranties or billable noncontract equipment owners.

5. Remember, customer relations and exceptional service determines whom the customer buys from.

6. It's not your job to sell, but to probe and ask questions to determine what the customer's needs are. Equipment types, usage, and customer industry are all factors in determining what contract solution is best for that customer.

7. The more critical the piece of equipment is to the customer's operation and success, the more the customer is willing to spend for contract coverage.

8. Excellent FSEs generate the most product-sales leads or blanket service-contract leads.

CHAPTER 11

INVENTORY MANAGEMENT

The necessary evil of field service! You are not alone if you don't like inventory. Most of us don't. Most would say it ranks up there with doing your tax forms. I agree; however, good inventory management practices are key to being a great FSE and certainly part of service management if you are interested in moving into service management.

My advice is to be great at inventory so that you can be great at service. A great mechanic keeps an organized and clean shop. A great FSE pays attention to detail on parts usage, transfers, returns, serial numbers, and other needs.

Without good inventory management practices, a company and the FSE cannot possibly provide effective service to their customers. Ineffective inventory practices lead to callbacks, delays, waste, troubleshooting difficulties, and frustration for all.

I always like to recognize that my company invests expensive materials and inventory in my skills and care to provide the best service levels possible to my customer. I have a responsibility to accurately account for this value, and it simply takes attention to detail and avoiding procrastination.

The easiest mistake to make with inventory is saying that you are in a hurry, but you will remember to do that later. Of course later always comes later...and so it goes.

My first practice in inventory management has been replaced with computers and service management systems. I was issued a black book with little tabs for each part number I stocked. Much like a checkbook register (before online banking), every usage, restock, and transfer was recorded with date, call number, and quantity. My manager would always ask to review my book. It traveled in my tool bag on every call along with my call report, and the entire call transaction was completed before leaving the customer's location. To this day, that is the correct practice, even though automation has greatly simplified this task.

So here it is, short and sweet.

- Keep up with your inventory at every single service call—before you leave the site. Details matter: quantity, serial numbers if required, damage, returns, and so on.
- View your inventory—and therefore your responsibility—as the tools to provide great service.
- Depending on your company's process, add value by seriously considering what exactly you need to stock and not stock to support your equipment and customer base. Geographic and response-time requirements matter, depending on your customer locations, requirements, and contract types.
- Service inventory is always about three things:
  1. dollar value of your stock
  2. turns ratio (or similar metrics like quantity on hand with usage)
  3. physical inventory variance (what is missing during inventory and is written off)
- Take pride in organizing and keeping your inventory cared for. Remember the last time you used that PCB in your stock for troubleshooting and didn't remember it had a problem before? I have done that to myself many times, and it makes for long evenings.

Inventory management goes hand in hand with productivity—it's operating in a quality manner. Stocking decisions, organizing and safeguarding of inventory, and accurate reporting all work to provide you an effective tool to maximize customer service.

Field Service 7
Inventory Management Action Items

1. Inventory management—stocking, care, usage records, replenishment, returns—is vital to productive FSE work.
2. Maintain inventory in your system every day. It's not like a checkbook register that you can put off.
3. Speaking of checks, inventory loss or scrap is like writing a check for your service operation. It's a real waste of funds that could be used for FSE hires, new equipment, new vehicles, more training, pay, and so on.
4. Inventory is part of the "triangle offense" for productivity—planning, decision making, and inventory.
5. Tedious but very important: We can't love everything about our job, can we?

CHAPTER 12

SELF-DEVELOPMENT

Field service engineers are professionals. They are experts in their field, product lines, and tools and must keep up with changing technology and applications. In addition to technology, FSEs have broad career opportunities to advance or to come in from the field for other roles within the company. As I said earlier, the field service industry is unique in all of the complementary functions that interface with field service. I have known many FSEs who were interested in customer service, engineering, contracts, product management, technical support and training, manufacturing, quality, safety, fleet, sales, marketing, and logistics.

Keep in mind that field sales and service personnel have a distinct advantage within their company. Those two functions are the customer-facing field representatives of the entire corporation. Many high-level executives have started their careers as field representatives and got to the executive level because of their skills in working directly with customers in the field, where the industry occurs (not back in an office), and have experience in promoting the brand of the entire corporation. I remember a CEO proudly proclaiming that if you are not in the field directly supporting a customer, then you need to be supporting someone who is. And yes, he had started as a field representative years ago.

I sincerely hope that you commit to an annual plan with your direct supervisor to address both the technology and your career interests. Every FSE must be engaged in technology development to prevent falling behind the technology changes that directly affect the systems you install and maintain. All of us, regardless of generation, can list major changes. In my time, I have seen, among other things:

- electronics—vacuum tubes to transistors to integrated circuits, EPROMS;
- pay phones (wasn't that a joy to call the office back in the day) to pagers to cell phones to texting to wearables;
- typewriters to computers to laptops to tablets to smart phones/apps, and now wearables;
- television to VHS/CD to DVD to streaming and downloaded music; and much more.

As professionals, you must keep learning, sharing, and developing your skills. Those skills, however, can also be shaped to your career interests. Field service engineering provides a gateway to many careers, depending on your interest, flexibility, and education or development. It's really up to you. Better yet, it doesn't always mean going back to school for degrees. Yes, sometimes engineering or business courses are required for a role you are interested in. You may choose to do that, and I bet your company offers tuition assistance to help you get there. But in many other cases, you have the opportunity to be mentored and involved in projects. On-the-job training opens doors for current employees who expressed an interest during the annual review.

First, establish a practice of conducting a casual self-assessment of your current product and technology knowledge each year. Step back and honestly ask yourself if you are the expert in the room based on your job assignments. This basis will allow you to begin planning what your technology training commitment will be for the upcoming year. Share this with your supervisor or technical specialist. You are essentially taking charge of your technical and professional development pathways.

Once you have done this for the technical side, then spend time reflecting on where you want to take your career. I always found driving time good for this exercise. One important point is not to just think of future career options, but as you do with your technology assessment, reflect on your status with the complete Field Service7. We all need to focus on the core elements to maximize our performance and potential as a field service engineer. I always need to add focus to one of these areas each and every year.

I hope you see the direction here to ground yourself in the Field Service 7 elements. By doing so, you will be rounded, focused, and energetic—the complete professional. I truly believe that this perspective and approach to your job will make you more fulfilled and accomplished as a field service engineer. This drives results, which enable you to be paid more, and it opens doors for many new opportunities.

CHAPTER 13

FIELD SERVICE7 REVIEW

P lease look at the Field Service7 as a balanced set of skills that are all necessary to optimize your performance in the job and provide advancement.

It's not that each of the Field Service7 elements are of the same weightage or importance but an FSE must demonstrate both commitment and proficiency in each one.

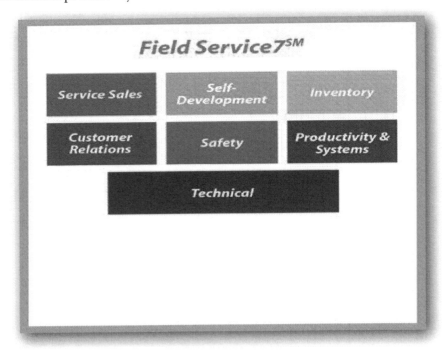

I suggest that you view the Field Service7 as a guideline and also as a continuum. It's a cycle which never stops, and that's actually a great thing. As mentioned earlier, we should never stop developing as an FSE, not only with the technology of the equipment you support, but also in the supporting skillsets of the Field Service7. For example, our productivity is heavily influenced by the mobile technology and apps that we use to process our calls or even to diagnose the equipment. Certainly that technology will continue to evolve. The same is true for service product creation and new and creative support contract programs that customer can choose from. I would never want my medical doctor to stop learning and developing or not understand all parts of his or her job to provide medical assistance. The same is true for the FSE profession.

I personally do not like things to be more complicated than they need to be, and the Field Service7 is a guideline that is very straightforward and will sustain as the service industry continues to evolve.

If you want to win, do the ordinary things better than anyone else does them day in and day out.

—Coach Chuck Noll

Rather than say the Field Service7 is ordinary, let's go with straightforward, but you get the point!

In Part III, you will hear first hand how being dedicated and balanced in all aspects of the FSE's job shaped each of the FSEs profiled and led to the career they desired.

PART III

PROFILES IN SERVICE

CHAPTER 14

INTRODUCTION—PROFILES IN SERVICE

I 've had the distinct privilege of working with hundreds of good field service engineers during my career. Some were role models and mentors; others were heroes to me when I was in management, and they saved the day; and many are friends after almost forty years of serving in the same industry.

The purpose of this chapter is to highlight their careers to give you some perspective on career prospects, backgrounds, skills, and insights.

This is also a special tribute to wonderful role models for us all. They were *intentional* about their FSE careers and how they led to opportunities and value-based lives.

To my profiled FSEs: Your stories beam your light for others to follow, and we are forever grateful!

———

Profile 1: Jim Jones
"I was born to be a field service engineer."
Background: senior field service engineer, field technical specialist, scientific instrument industry

Jim was the first FSE I learned from who stated that his goal for every service call was to satisfy the customer, not just fix the instrument.

I met Jim in 1979 while I was a junior-level field service engineer working on scientific instruments for Beckman Instruments (later Beckman Coulter). Jim was a senior FSE with primary responsibility for the liquid scintillation and gamma counters (nuclear product line) that Beckman manufactured. Almost forty years later I can still clearly recall his mastery of all models within the Beckman nuclear line. He became my lifeline and mentor as I learned the products but most important, the FSE profession.

What stood out for me about Jim was his total command of and love for the FSE job. And after over forty years, he's still an FSE but for his own company as an independent service organization. Jim taught me the importance of interpersonal relationships and taking the monkey off the customer's back. I would tell the customer that I was putting the 'monkey' on my back and only he/she could take it off.

> "And that I was their personal FSE until the problem is solved to their satisfaction, but once that was done I would go back to my account and assigned systems."

As we have discussed, customers are a critical element to the Field Service7. Jim has always invested time in understanding what his customers do and what's important to their scientific research. By knowing about his customers and their science, he has both empathy as well as creative ideas to satisfy his customers or solve problems. Let me give you an example that will also serve to support the earlier business point about the importance of field service engineering to a corporation.

Besides Jim's daily service responsibilities, at Beckman he also had a formal job role as the account specialist for one of his district's largest accounts, the University of Maryland. The account specialist role at Beckman was basically to represent all aspects of service for Beckman at the account, even though the FSE would work on only a fraction of the models installed at the account. In other words, the account specialist was responsible for all work done at the account by himself and other FSEs who worked there. And it fell to him to grow the service contract volume.

At one point, Beckman was trying to reduce its service cost for the service contracts and provide better value to the customer and maintain a competitive edge. Jim did a complete cost analysis and determined that during one particular time of the year the service cost would increase well above the other months' averages. After reviewing the data and root causes, Jim determined that it was a seasonal impact of new medical students working in the lab at the beginning of a semester. Further, Jim concluded, these students were not trained in the basics of instrument operation and theory. So Jim proposed a short training seminar at various times of the week (free of charge) to help the students with basic instrument operations, which freed up the teaching and lab staff for their other duties. Sure enough, service costs were lowered, students were better trained and happier, and best yet, both the university and Beckman were more than satisfied with reduced downtime and service costs—a classic win-win situation. Now, my point in all of this is to show how Jim's understanding of the customer's business and specifics enabled him to effectively identify the root issue and create a solution that all parties benefited from.

Jim's command in front of the customer is a work of art. Too often FSEs rush to the downed equipment and start troubleshooting. They do not get a good start to truly diagnosing the problem. Jim starts with putting his tool bag down. He listens to everyone involved to get an understanding of the problem they are having. It's really just like an effective sales process of first asking questions and discovering what their needs are. We have always heard that God gave us two ears and one mouth— use them accordingly.

Jim's approach is calming during a heated discussion of, say, a repeating failure with perhaps lost samples or experiments, and it also establishes a baseline to resolve the expressed problem areas. In technical troubleshooting, you really need all the clues and observed problems to effectively diagnose the problem. As Jim puts it, this is also his chance to let the customer vent steam, and it gives him a chance to express complete confidence that he has the problem on his shoulders to fix. In other words, the customer now has confidence that the problem will be solved to his or her complete satisfaction.

At Beckman, we often heard that the reason the customer would buy Beckman was not low cost or product features, but complete confidence in service and support. We were proud to be the best-trained and the highest-quality service professionals in the industry.

Jim was telling me that you have to be happy at what you do. Just today, Jim was telling me he was "born to be an FSE." He absolutely loves his work in solving problems for his customers. My personal belief is that Jim has not just demonstrated the Field Service7 but also has helped to define it within his industry.

In summary, Jim Jones is a leading example of someone who loves the industry. Jim left Beckman and worked as a senior field specialist in both direct service and training other FSEs and application specialists for highly technical mass spectrophotometers. He now continues as a sole proprietor of a small scientific instrument service business where he can still practice his craft.

Jim's advice to us in the industry is to have a practice of "partnering" new FSEs with a small staff of senior FSEs to teach the profession—not just the technical aspects of the products, but the other critical components of the Field Service7.

Profile 2: Jennifer Schonher
"The problem solver"

Background: field service engineer, team leader, service automation project leader, customer support business process consultant, director systems support—scientific instruments, CRM, and Internet security industries

Jennifer is a high-energy go-getter, a do-it-all woman with whom I worked at Beckman Instruments/Beckman Coulter. She later moved on to other careers based on her field service experience.

Although she doesn't say these words, Jennifer is someone who—if you made the mistake of saying no or offering a lame response to an idea she had—would ask, "Why not?"

I always had a feeling she used the same self-talk to challenge herself to have both a career and a family. As a ball of energy and aspirations, Jennifer demonstrated how as an FSE you can leverage those responsibilities and experiences for new and different type of work.

Jennifer graduated from the University of Vermont with a bachelor's degree in electrical engineering, and when she landed in San Francisco after graduation, her first job after college was as a field service engineer. She serviced the liquid chromatograph product line and capillary electrophoresis lines for Beckman.

I got to know Jennifer after she had worked in the field for a number of years and was named to be part of a field advisory group to management. This was the time I first witnessed the why-not challenge. She consistently provided constructive feedback on how to improve our service delivery for different products to enhance the customer experience and improve company profits.

Jennifer tells of the years of shaping her development as an FSE. She clearly saw her value as a "problem solver" for her customers. Years later, when she was asked to speak at the University of Vermont School of Engineering commencement ceremony, she told the story about her first career as an FSE problem solver, and led her listeners to consider being problem solvers in their careers to add value. The FSE as "problem solver" is a constant theme across all successful FSEs and among my profiled FSE group.

You see, as a self-described problem solver, Jennifer was practicing the elements of the Field Service7 in always being prepared and approaching customer relations and service sales by solving each customer's problem. Jennifer contributes her career development to working in different environments each day, with different customer personalities, different products, and the opportunity to work independently. She valued the direct responsibility for a customer problem and the ensuing opportunities. Her customers relied on her and paid good money for their service contracts, and she built confidence and account relationships a little each day.

I love Jennifer's outlook. Over the years she was faced with complex technical, customer account, and internal team operational challenges. She learned not to fear mistakes, and even take risks with earned empowerment within her organization. When she considers risks, Jennifer says, "Ask yourself, 'What is the worst that can happen?'" Usually, defining the worst thing that could happen guided her to adjust her plans and move forward. After these years of working as an FSE, she was confident in her career, having grown from a technical position to an account manager and service team leader.

Jennifer credits the opportunity to work in the field directly with customers and solving problems as the key stepping stone to her future career options. Jennifer cites her daily self-talk, "I can do this," as the necessary energy and direction to move forward as an intentional field service engineer. I believe Jennifer's energy and self-motivating standard to grow and try new things was undoubtedly a perfect match of her intelligence and education, coupled with a career in field service.

As she moved her career into software project management, customer care strategy, and technical management, she never lost that customer-centric insight. She always used the FSE experiences of working with multiple personalities. Jennifer credits these field service experiences to first involving her in internal projects and later with different jobs. Jennifer once stated to me that she rather enjoyed a little discomfort and pressure in her daily work, and we know as FSEs that this is often the case. That edge has helped her prosper today in a new career.

Jennifer lives well outside of work, and she has mastered the ability to live an intentional life with family, work, travel, and a quest for the new and interesting opportunities life can bring. Nothing is small with Jennifer; she always makes big moves. She walked out of the college graduation hall to return twenty years later as the commencement speaker. Her secret? Be a problem solver!

Profile 3: Tom Erbach
"The job maker and people builder"

Background: US Navy electronic technician, chemist, field service engineer, field applications specialist, national training specialist, applications and training manager, field development manager, and business consultant.

While I've always joked with Tom that he could never keep a job, he worked for one company for thirty years and held many new and challenging roles based on his start as a field service engineer. As Tom says, "I've always invented my own job." How true it is! I worked with Tom for over ten years. He was also a problem solver like Jennifer and actually created unique roles within a Fortune 500 corporation to solve some critical organizational development problems.

A driving influence on Tom was his experience in working directly with customers on chemistry-based instrumentation. Besides the various personalities and situations, he observed how the company's past support model wasn't appropriate for the different chemistry-based instruments. As he gained experience on the product line, he became the go-to FSE in his region. Remember the point in the Field Service7 about technical skills and fully mastering the product line to be the expert in the room? Well, that was Tom, and he also had an advantage with his background in chemistry.

Tom spent extra time initiating a new troubleshooting model and later FSE training, and convinced his regional management to formalize the project to improve the effectiveness of the service call and the customer experience. This project launched Tom's career from FSE to manager of a nationwide training group for over 250 FSEs.

I attribute much of Tom's success to his ability to listen to the end-user customer, fellow FSEs, tech support, and management to clearly identify the root cause of the problem. Tom also provided advice to other FSEs to be part of the solution—the powerful advice in not just observing and diagnosing as some FSEs do, but to also use one's energy in a productive manner to help or lead in solving the problem, instead of sitting on the sidelines and complaining. I can attest as a manager that our biggest project successes came from FSEs, service coordinators, and other frontline employees who did what Tom did to be part of the solution and not the problem. Definitely words to live by!

Another great insight from Tom is that as an FSE, you should keep the customer perspective front and center at all times. He says, "Recognize what customers want and how to deliver it to them." Tom's customer centricity drove our organization to redefine, challenge, and improve the customer support model—despite enormous internal resistance. Ultimately, profits were higher, FSE training and development was improved, and obviously, the customer was better served.

I have chosen to highlight Tom's experiences and insights to reinforce the FSE's role as it relates to improving business outcomes and also to creating future career opportunities.

Tom spent thirty years with a Fortune 500 company that was headquartered in Southern California. In those days, it was typical for an employee to relocate to move up in the organization. Tom started and ended his thirty-year career based at the same regional office in Chicago, which was Tom's preference for his family. He held national roles and worked closely with corporate technical support and training, human resources, manufacturing, sales and marketing, and other functions. In today's world, there is much opportunity with virtual linking to these functions if that is your preference.

Tom would agree that his roles were all challenging and filled with obstacles. He quotes Henry Ford: "Failure is just another way to move forward with new information."

My advice is to make sure you strive for what interests you and that you work in a company environment that values new ideas and experimentation. This also applies to your direct supervisor, a person who values the rewards of failure and self-development.

Tom's favorite parts of the FSE job included troubleshooting, problem solving, and taking sometimes frustrated customers and turning them around. When they were able to confidently get back to their operation and production, he was satisfied in his work. I appreciate Tom's insight, personal character, and drive to take care of the customer, which has served him well as an FSE and other key roles in his career.

Profile 4: Scott Anderson
"Master Scaleman, complete sales-service professional"

Background: certified welder, manufacturing assembler, fabricator, self-taught electronics technician, master-scaleman credential, field service technician, and area sales manager

Scott currently works at Fairbanks Scales in a unique role as both a field service technician and sales manager. In this role, he splits his time between servicing and selling major industrial weighing systems. Scott has been with Fairbanks Scales for thirty-eight years, and before joining Fairbanks as a field service technician, he was a fabricator for another scale manufacturer. Scott started his career as an assembly worker and then learned welding during night school and became a certified welder and led the fabrication of new scale systems in the factory. He was doing well in the factory, but he was curious about installing the scales he built and servicing those scales in the field. That's when he joined Fairbanks and left the factory for a career in field service.

Today, Scott services advanced computer-controlled weighing systems in the Northern Ohio area, including automated systems for unattended operation and other advanced instrument systems. He is largely self-trained on the electronics, having completed many factory product courses and outside course work to advance his skills.

He earned the prestigious weighing systems credential of master scaleman and has been named top tech numerous times as well as employee of the year. As the company's sole combo role of both sales and service, his skills in customer relations and service selling of the Field Service7 have served him well to be promoted to this unique role.

He reflects that on his job, no two days are ever the same, and it never gets boring. Scott takes personal pride in problem solving and developing customer relationships. He will be the first to tell you that he doesn't sell to people; he provides support and options to his customers. Nor does he need to discount much or even have a lot of competition because he provides the ultimate value in trust and confidence to his customers.

Scott stresses the importance of one-to-one communications and enthusiasm for what you do for a living. Handling difficult situations with multiple internal company personalities is critical as an FSE. He credits his skills as a service technician as the basis for his sales responsibility and successes.

Scott explains further that with the independence and responsibility techs have in their job, there is a lot they can get accomplished in a five-day workweek. He really appreciates the nature of the job independence and being responsible for making both scheduling and on-site decisions. He recalls the days when he worked in a factory setting and making his daily visits to industrial facilities, and compares the freedom and independence of his job as a field service tech. Scott takes great satisfaction from his customer account relationships and the fact that he solves problems and can reap immediate satisfaction in his work. Scott says he is young in the industry after forty years, with ever-changing technology, the various customer relationships and facilities, and how field service is always changing.

Scott observes that there is going to be a huge gap in the field service workforce with the pending retirements. He encourages technicians who are considering this field to be eager and seek a job with freedom and independence. "There is enormous responsibility in the service technician's role that comes with the independence and working as a self-managed service professional. The industry needs new enthusiastic talent—people who are willing to learn and constantly adapt."

I've had the honor to be the leader of Scott's service organization at Fairbanks, and I and many others take great pleasure and pride seeing Scott Anderson at work, devoted to his customers, profession, and company. The field service network needs more Scott Andersons out there making their way as true professionals and having fulfilling and rewarding careers.

SUMMARY

M y intention for writing this book was twofold: (1) to attract new talent into the field service profession and (2) to provide a framework for professional development as a field service engineer.

We started by describing what a wonderful career choice field service engineering is and the opportunities that exist to advance. The independence and responsibility that come with the job are rich in experiences. I can cite so many stories from my travels and interactions with people over the years, and I credit them to an interesting job. Second, field service engineering is the science of technology matched with the art of customer service. I have loved it!

The Field Service7 is a program to follow that will align your skills as an FSE with the company and its service organization's performance results. You should never underestimate your contributions to the company's success.

I believe we should all live our lives with intention to maximize our value on earth. Einstein said, "Live a life of value, not of importance." Since it is safe to assume that FSEs are generally not celebrities, I probably didn't offend anyone with Einstein's quote! My hope is that you will be attracted to this profession and that you choose to be an intentional field service engineer.

I can assure you that as an intentional field service engineer, you will prosper based on your success by dedicating your development and performance to the Field Service7 framework.

Now it is up to you to take action and take control of your destiny. The FSEs profiled in this book are inspirational and represent various paths they chose to take for their careers, based on being intentional and mastering the seven critical skills of a field service engineer. I hope you take their lead and follow with your own intentional career.

Finally, I encourage you to sign up for the free FSE website, dedicated to our profession and its opportunities: www.fieldservicegrid.com.

With the first printing of this book, the website is just beginning, so I ask that you consider being one of our first groups of members. The free member site will include additional Field Service7 information and links to training and member forums to discuss opportunities and careers.

Again, my friends—congratulations for your interest and dedication to be the complete professional FSE. I am grateful that you chose to read this book, and I would like to help you in your career development as an intentional field service engineer. Go tell your boss or prospective employers that you are an intentional field service engineer, and then tell them the story.

Field Service Grid

Development-Opportunity-Results

50622909R00052

Made in the USA
Columbia, SC
09 February 2019